The GIANT ANIMALS Series™

Rhinos

Marianne Johnston

The Rosen Publishing Group's
PowerKids Press™
New York

Published in 1997 by The Rosen Publishing Group, Inc.
29 East 21st Street, New York, NY 10010

First Edition

Book Design: Kim Sonsky

Photo Credits: Front and back cover and page 4 © Ronn Maratea/International Stock; p. 7 © Chad Ehlers/International Stock; pp. 8, 13 © Wildlife Conservation Society headquartered @ The New York Zoologocal Society; pp. 11, 16 © Michele & Tom Grimm/International Stock; p. 12 © Bruce Mathews/MIDWESTOCK; p. 14 © 1996 PhotoDisc, Inc.; p. 18 © Raid Planete Poussie/Gamma Liason; p. 21 © Michael P. Manheim/MIDWESTOCK.

Johnston, Marianne.
    Rhinos / Marianne Johnston.
        p.   cm. — (The giant animals series)
    Includes index.
    Summary: Examines the physical characteristics, habits, and natural environment of the five species of rhinoceros, two of which are found in Africa and three in Asia.
    ISBN 0-8239-5144-8 (lib. bdg.)
    1. Rhinoceroses—Juvenile literature. [1. Rhinoceroses. 2. Endangered species.] I. Title. II. Series: Johnston, Marianne. Giant animals series.
QL737.U63J64 1996
5999.66'8—dc21   96-37465
                                                                      CIP
                                                                       AC

Manufactured in the United States of America

CONTENTS

RHINOCEROSES

A rhinoceros, or rhino, is a large animal that has very thick skin and **hooves** (HOOVZ) on its feet. There are five different **species** (SPEE-sheez), or kinds, of rhinos in the world. Two kinds live in Africa and three kinds live in Asia.

The black rhino and the white rhino live on the **savannas** (suh-VAN-uhz) of Africa.

The Javan rhino, the Sumatran rhino, and the great Indian rhino live in the **rain forests** (RAYN FOR-ests) of Asia. There are about 11,000 rhinos in the world.

◀ African rhinos live on the grassy savannas of Africa.

5

AFRICAN RHINOS

The white rhino is the largest kind of African rhino. It can be six feet tall at the shoulder and thirteen feet long. These rhinos can weigh up to 5,000 pounds. Many white rhinos live in southern Africa.

The black rhino is a little smaller than the white rhino. This rhino lives in eastern and southern Africa.

Even though they are named the black rhino and the white rhino, both of these kinds of rhinos have gray-colored skin.

African rhinos have thick, hairless skin. ▶

ASIAN RHINOS

Asian rhinos live in forests instead of on savannas. The great Indian rhino is the largest of the Asian rhinos. This rhino lives in India and Nepal.

.

The Javan rhino is the shyest of all the rhinos. It lives in the forests of Java, which is part of Indonesia.

The smallest of the rhinos is the Sumatran, which lives in Indonesia, Malaysia, and Indochina. Its red hair is very thick. It is the only kind of rhino with hair.

◀ The Sumatran rhino has thick hair that looks like fur.

WHAT DO RHINOS EAT?

Rhinos are **herbivores** (HER-bih-vohrz). This means they only eat plants.

The white rhino and the great Indian rhino are **grazers** (GRAY-zerz). They eat grass and small plants. The wide shape of the white rhino's lips makes grazing easy.

The other three kinds of rhinos are **browsers** (BROW-zerz). They eat twigs, leaves, and small trees. The black rhino uses its hooked lip to grab leaves and branches and rip them off the plant.

African rhinos eat grass and small plants on the ground. ▶

10

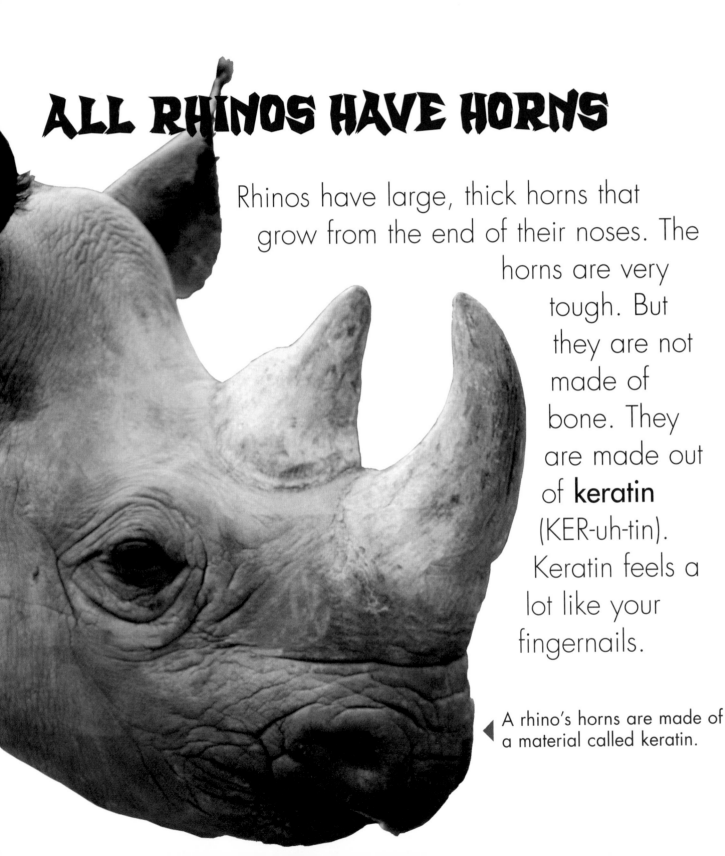

ALL RHINOS HAVE HORNS

Rhinos have large, thick horns that grow from the end of their noses. The horns are very tough. But they are not made of bone. They are made out of **keratin** (KER-uh-tin). Keratin feels a lot like your fingernails.

◀ A rhino's horns are made of a material called keratin.

If a rhino's horn is broken off in a fight or by humans, it will grow back, just like a fingernail. The African rhinos and the Sumatran rhino have two horns. The biggest one is in the front. The Javan and the great Indian rhinos only have one horn.

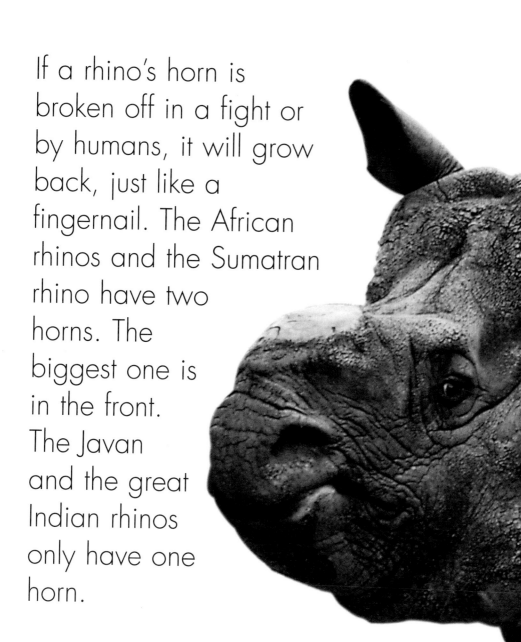

If a rhino's horn is broken off, it will grow back over time. ▶

13

YOUNG RHINOS

When a baby rhino is born, it can weigh up to 150 pounds. That's as much as a grown-up human might weigh!

Baby rhinos grow very fast. By the time they are one year old, they weigh 1,500 pounds. And that's only half as big as a full-grown rhino!

Baby rhinos, or **calves** (KAVS), follow their mothers very closely for the first three days. Moms and their calves stay together for about two to four years, until the next baby is born.

◀ A baby rhino will stay with its mother until the next baby is born. Then the older calf goes off on its own.

15

SENSES

Rhinos do not have good eyesight. A rhino's eyes are on either side of its head. That makes it hard for a rhino to see anything right in front of it. A rhino can't even see something as big as a person from ten feet away.

To make up for its bad eyesight, a rhino will use its excellent sense of smell to learn about its **environment** (en-VY-ron-ment). The rhino also uses its sharp sense of hearing.

Although it has poor eyesight, the rhino has ▶ excellent hearing and sense of smell.

WALLOWING

Rhinos like to **wallow** (WAH-loh), or roll around, in mud. A rhino will find a river or a small pool of water in which to roll around. Wallowing in mud or muddy water keeps the rhino cool in the hot sun.

Great Indian rhinos like to stay in the water for long periods of time. They are great swimmers. African rhinos just get in the water, roll around in the mud, and then get out again.

The mud is helpful in another way. It dries on the rhino's skin and makes it harder for bugs to bite the rhino.

◀ Wallowing in the mud keeps the rhino's skin from getting too hot.

19

RHINOS AND HUMANS

Humans have been the worst enemy of rhinos. Humans travel to Africa and kill rhinos for their horns. In Asia, the horns are crushed into powder and used for medicine.

In a country called Yemen, the horns are carved into handles for special knives. These knives are signs of power.

Humans have killed so many rhinos that they have become an **endangered species** (en-DAYN-jehrd SPEE-sheez). This means that since there are so few rhinos left they are close to becoming **extinct** (ex-TEENKT).

At the Okanagan Game Farm in Canada, rhinos are cared for and protected by humans. ▶

20

RHINOS TODAY

In 1980 there were 20,000 black rhinos in the African country of Kenya. Now there are only 500. African **governments** (GUV-ern-ments) have passed laws to protect rhinos. Now, in most parts of Africa, it is against the law to kill rhinos. People who break this law are called **poachers** (POH-cherz).

The only rhino that is not endangered is the white rhino.

We can see and learn more about rhinos in zoos and wildlife parks, where some of them live. If enough people learn and care about the rhinos, one day they may be taken off the endangered species list.

GLOSSARY

browser (BROW-zer) An animal that eats leaves, twigs, and branches from trees and small plants.

calf (KAF) A young animal.

endangered species (en-DAYN-jehrd SPEE-sheez) A kind of animal that has very few of its kind left.

environment (en-VY-ron-ment) The area where something lives.

extinct (ex-TEENKT) When a certain kind of animal does not exist anymore.

government (GUV-ern-ment) The people who rule a state or country.

grazer (GRAY-zer) An animal that eats grass and plants from the ground.

herbivore (HER-bih-vohr) An animal that eats only plants.

hoof (HOOF) A hard, horn-like covering on the feet of animals.

keratin (KER-uh-tin) A very hard material that makes up the rhino's horns. It feels a lot like fingernails.

poacher (POH-cher) A person who kills certain animals, even though it is against the law.

rain forest (RAYN FOR-est) A very wet area that has many kinds of plants, trees, and animals.

savanna (suh-VAN-uh) Large area of grassy land.

species (SPEE-sheez) A group of living things that have some of the same features.

wallow (WAH-loh) When an animal rolls around in mud or a pool of water.

23

INDEX